BUILD BACK BETTER SECTOR GUIDES
VOLUME 6: POWER

OCTOBER 2024

ASIAN DEVELOPMENT BANK

CONTENTS

TABLES AND BOXES

Tables

Boxes

ACKNOWLEDGMENTS

Preparation of this *Build Back Better Sector Guides* series was led by Belinda Hewitt, senior disaster risk management specialist, Climate Change and Sustainable Development Department (CCSD), ADB with substantive inputs and review from Brigitte Balthasar, senior disaster and climate risk financing specialist, CCSD, ADB; Charlotte Benson, former principal disaster risk management Specialist, ADB; Alexandra Galperin, unit head, disaster risk management, CCSD, ADB; Steven Goldfinch, senior disaster risk management specialist, CCSD, ADB; Anne Orquiza, senior disaster risk management officer, CCSD, ADB; Grendel Saldevar, senior operations assistant, CCSD, ADB; and Mario Unterwaining, former disaster risk management specialist (resilient infrastructure), ADB. The series was developed in close collaboration with ADB Sectors Group and country teams. Margie Peters-Fawcett copy edited the volumes with the assistance of Cherry Lynn Zafaralla as proofreader. Layout was created by Rommel Marilla, page proofs checking by Levi Rodolfo Lusterio, and administrative support by Michelle Imperial.

This volume was authored by David von Hippel and Glen Platt with inputs from David Elzinga, principal energy specialist (climate change); Lyndree Malang, consultant; Darshak Mehta, consultant; and Kee-Yung Nam, principal energy economist from ADB Sectors Group. Case studies on the recovery of Tonga's power systems following Tropical Cyclone Gita were developed with guidance from Setitaia Pasivaka Chen and Vijay Narayan, former senior project officer, Pacific Department, ADB. Peer review by Amir Gilani of Miyamoto International and Rachael Jonassen is greatly appreciated.

ABBREVIATIONS

ADB	Asian Development Bank
BBB	build back better
DMC	developing member country
EAL	Emergency Assistance Loan
PDNA	post-disaster needs assessment
T&D	transmission and distribution
TC Gita	Tropical Cyclone Gita
TPL	Tonga Power Ltd.

Following the 2004 Asian tsunami, Sulaiman Daud, Aceh Power Sector Manager, was in the frontline after the tsunami, working for months with his crew to restore electricity to the province in Indonesia.

A woman from Singla village extracts her belongings from the rubble in the aftermath of the 2015 earthquake in Nepal.

I

INTRODUCTION

Timely support for recovery and reconstruction efforts is critical when a disaster occurs to minimize any potential long-term setbacks to sustainable and inclusive socioeconomic development. It is essential to provide a window of opportunity to rebuild assets and improve livelihoods to increase climate and disaster resilience and reduce the risk of future hazards. With impacts of disasters projected to rise in the coming decades as affected by climate change, unplanned urbanization, poor risk governance, and a range of other trends, challenges relating to climate uncertainty, growing complexity of infrastructure systems, and the compounding nature of multiple hazard events underline the importance of ensuring that communities and infrastructure systems are equipped to cope, adapt, and recover when faced with future shocks and stresses.

Developing member countries (DMCs) of the Asian Development Bank (ADB) bear a disproportionate share of impacts from geophysical and extreme weather hazard events. Between 2004 and 2023, these DMCs accounted for 55% of global disaster fatalities and 74% of people affected.[1] Over this 20-year period, ADB has provided more than $9.1 billion in financing for emergency assistance loan (EAL) projects relating to disasters triggered by natural hazards, conflict, displacement, food insecurity, and health emergencies. The support that ADB offers its DMCs aims at ensuring resilient post-disaster recovery, as well as strengthening long-term disaster risk reduction.

ADB's Strategy 2030[2] and 2021 Disaster and Emergency Assistance Policy[3] outline commitments to ensure effective response and support to build back better (BBB) after a disaster or emergency.[4] "Build back better" refers to the use of the early recovery and reconstruction phases after a disaster or emergency to increase resilience of nations and communities to future events by integrating risk reduction

---

1   Centre for Research on the Epidemiology of Disasters, EM-DAT: The International Disaster Database. www.emdat.be (accessed 5 February 2024). People affected by multiple disasters have been counted multiple times.

2   Asian Development Bank (ADB). 2017. *Strategy 2030: Achieving a Prosperous, Inclusive, Resilient, and Sustainable Asia and the Pacific.*

3   ADB. 2021. *Revised Disaster and Emergency Assistance Policy.*

4   Strategy 2030 sets out a commitment to "provide assistance for disaster response, including support to build back better."

measures into the restoration of physical infrastructure, societal systems, livelihoods, economies, and the environment.[5] By systematically promoting risk-informed, well-designed, and timely recovery and reconstruction, ADB supports the implementation of international agreements, such as the Sendai Framework for Disaster Risk Reduction 2015–2030 and the 2030 Agenda for Sustainable Development Goals, including its 17 Sustainable Development Goals, both of which promote a comprehensive approach toward disaster risk management and BBB frameworks, including through community-based applications.

The six volumes that comprise the *Build Back Better Sector Guides* series aim to support ADB staff, consultants, and DMC counterparts to enhance the climate and disaster resilience of DMC communities, infrastructure, and systems through effective and well-designed post-disaster assistance. The volumes are based on principles, measures, and lessons learned from the international BBB literature; a review of over 40 ADB EALs processed between 2004 and 2021; and the outcome of consultations with a wide range of ADB staff.

Each of the volumes has been co-developed with relevant ADB sector and thematic groups. The sectors are areas in which ADB has played a key role in post-disaster recovery and reconstruction and where majority of ADB's disaster and emergency assistance has focused in the last 20 years. They are as follows:

(i)   Volume 1: Overview
(ii)   Volume 2: Transport
(iii)   Volume 3: Water, Sanitation, and Hygiene (WASH)
(iv)   Volume 4: Irrigated Agriculture
(v)   Volume 5: Social Infrastructure
(vi)   Volume 6: Power

This Volume 6: Power provides an overview of good practice solutions, considerations, and lessons learned for building back better for power systems, but does not represent a general or step-by-step handbook on methods to prepare and implement post-disaster needs assessment (PDNA) or EALs; nor does it for other forms of post-disaster assistance.

The scope of this series includes building resilience in response to disasters triggered by natural hazards; however, some of its content is relevant to the broader aspect of economic recovery, including within the context of health emergencies and conflict. Complementary objectives, including equity and inclusion, green recovery, poverty reduction, and broader sustainable development, are also presented.

---

[5]   Adapted from United Nations General Assembly. 2016. Report of the Open-Ended Intergovernmental Expert Working Group on Indicators and Terminology Relating to DRR. Seventy-First Session, Item 19(c).

ADB's Role in Resilient Post-Disaster Recovery and Reconstruction

Following a disaster, ADB can mobilize rapid post-disaster technical support under the second window of its Asia Pacific Disaster Response Fund in areas such as the preparation of PDNAs; government-led recovery plans; and post-disaster projects, including EALs. The PDNA is a well-established tailored methodology that is used for analyzing damage, loss, and needs prioritization. While the exercise should be led by the government, it is often conducted with the support of one or more international partners. The PDNA compiles information relating to the physical impacts of a disaster, economic value of damages and losses, human and macroeconomic impacts, and cost of early and long-term recovery needs and priorities. As such, the PDNA is an important tool to inform implementation of BBB through post-disaster programming.

Once recovery and reconstruction requirements have been assessed, ADB can mobilize finance for recovery and reconstruction through EAL, additional financing for pre-established projects, and investment projects that support longer-term reconstruction needs. ADB's 2021 Emergency Assistance Loan Policy enables the rapid approval of loans (within 12 weeks) to assist in the rebuilding of high-priority physical assets and the restoration of economic, social, and governance activities following disasters triggered by natural hazards, health emergencies, food insecurity, technological and industrial accidents, and post-conflict situations.[6] The Emergency Assistance Loan Policy and Disaster and Emergency Assistance Policy aim to support DMC's BBB efforts to enhance climate and disaster resilience. Table 1 provides a list of additional resources relating to ADB's policies and directives relating to post-disaster assistance.

Table 1: Key Documents on ADB Policies and Guidance for Post-Disaster Assistance

Document	Web Page
2021 Disaster and Emergency Assistance Policy	https://www.adb.org/documents/revised-disaster-and-emergency-assistance-policy
Revised Emergency Assistance Loan Policy	https://www.adb.org/documents/revised-emergency-assistance-loan-policy
Establishment of a Second Window of Assistance under the Asia Pacific Disaster Response Fund	https://www.adb.org/documents/establishment-second-window-assistance-under-asia-pacific-disaster-response-fund
Post-Disaster Needs Assessment Guidelines	https://www.recoveryplatform.org/pdna
Disaster Recovery Planning: Explanatory Note and Case Study	https://www.adb.org/publications/disaster-recovery-planning-explanatory-note-case-study

Source: Asian Development Bank.

---

6   ADB. 2021. *Revised Emergency Assistance Loan Policy*.

Importance of Long-Term Resilience Building

Long-term and upstream approaches to resilience building are critical to minimize the impacts of disasters and ensure more effective and efficient use of post-disaster assistance resources. ADB can play a key role in leveraging increased risk awareness to ensure resilience-focused upstream planning. Where risk-responsive socioeconomic development and sector plans are already in place ahead of a disaster, they can more effectively guide long-term disaster recovery and bring about a shift toward resilience and sustainable development.

Risk-informed sector plans enable more rapid and effective post-disaster recovery and reconstruction where they are informed by comprehensive multihazard disaster risk assessments and incorporate ex ante recovery planning. Past ADB EALs, such as the 2015 Nepal: Earthquake Emergency Assistance Project (see Volume 5: Social Infrastructure) and the 2018 Tonga: Cyclone Gita Recovery Project (section III-I), aligned recovery planning with climate and disaster resilience objectives set out in existing sector programs, government road maps, and the national development plan.

Use of the Build Back Better Sector Guides

This sector guide is intended to be read in conjunction with the introductory "Build Back Better Sector Guide Volume 1: Overview." The overview guide covers the broad measures that are likely relevant to any post-disaster recovery and reconstruction project, regardless of sector.

While this volume does not provide detailed technical guidance, it does provide various additional technical resources that can guide project-specific decision-making (Appendix: Suggested Readings). For any given power sector project, it is important that resilience measures are selected appropriately and on a project-by-project basis, informed by an understanding of the relevant power system components and local context. There should be analysis of current and future risk; economic development objectives; economic feasibility and viability; as well as relevant policies, including climate and disaster risk management and safeguards requirements.

ADB funded eight power supply and distribution projects in six districts in Aceh, Indonesia after the 2004 Asian tsunami.

ADB Federated States of Micronesia: Yap Renewable Energy Development Project (44469-013).
The project included three 275-kilowatt demountable wind turbines that can be tilted to the ground
ahead of an extreme weather event and thus avoid damage.

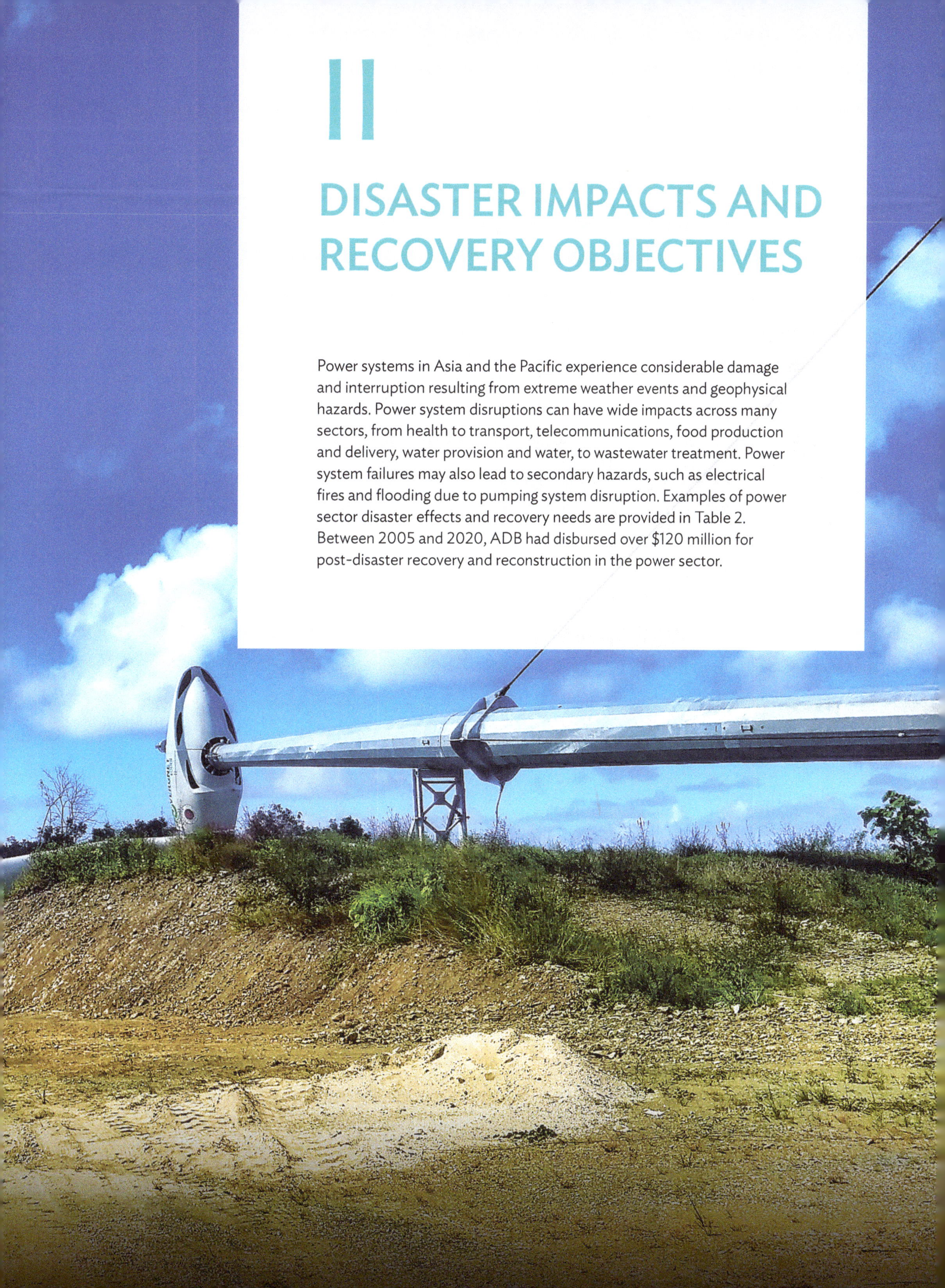

II

DISASTER IMPACTS AND RECOVERY OBJECTIVES

Power systems in Asia and the Pacific experience considerable damage and interruption resulting from extreme weather events and geophysical hazards. Power system disruptions can have wide impacts across many sectors, from health to transport, telecommunications, food production and delivery, water provision and water, to wastewater treatment. Power system failures may also lead to secondary hazards, such as electrical fires and flooding due to pumping system disruption. Examples of power sector disaster effects and recovery needs are provided in Table 2. Between 2005 and 2020, ADB had disbursed over $120 million for post-disaster recovery and reconstruction in the power sector.

Table 2: Examples of Significant Power Sector Disaster Effects and Recovery Needs

Event	Disaster Effects (damages and losses, $ million)		Recovery Needs ($ million)	
	Infrastructure[a]	Power Sector	Infrastructure[a]	Power Sector
Floods (Pakistan), 2010[b]	1,746	309 (18%)	2,556	106 (4%)
Earthquake (Nepal), 2015[b]	652	207 (32%)	743	186 (25%)
Tropical Cyclone Gita (Tonga), 2018[b]	13	8 (62%)	47	45 (96%)
Floods (Pakistan), 2022[b]	4,323	91 (2%)	5,438	117 (2%)

[a] Infrastructure damages and losses are defined based on the post-disaster needs assessment guidelines produced by the Global Fund for Disaster Reconstruction and Recovery (GFDRR. 2013. *Post-Disaster Needs Assessments: Guidelines—Volume A: Guidelines*). These guidelines include the water and sanitation, community infrastructure, energy, transport, and telecommunications sectors.

[b] Government of Pakistan, ADB, and World Bank. 2010. *Pakistan Floods 2010: Preliminary Damage and Needs Assessment.* Islamabad; Government of Nepal. 2015. *Nepal Earthquake 2015: Post Disaster Needs Assessment—Vol. A: Key Findings.* Kathmandu; Government of Tonga. 2018. *Post Disaster Rapid Assessment: Tropical Cyclone Gita, February 12, 2018*; and Government of Pakistan et. al. 2022. *Pakistan Floods 2022: Post-Disaster Needs Assessment.*

Note: This table provides a selection of examples where power sector disaster effects comprised a high proportion of recovery investment needs following different natural hazard events. Where required values were not available, amounts in local currency were converted to United States dollars based on the exchange rate for the event year. Source: World Bank. World Development Indicators (accessed 1 June 2023).

Source: Asian Development Bank.

Contemporary power systems in ADB's DMCs are particularly vulnerable to natural hazards; although they may supply electricity to customers over long distances, power generation components are usually centralized. In addition, many power systems include a combination of aging components and newer infrastructure that are not effectively integrated with each other. Power systems in DMCs also may lack modern, streamlined control systems that are designed to effectively dispatch backup power during disaster recovery. A loss of major power plants or major electricity loads such as large buildings or factories—particularly in the presence of damage to the transmission and distribution system—risks a cascade of power outages due to overload. System-wide failures will occur if there is a failure at any central point of the system (such as generation, substation, or transmission and distribution); should it do so in a core component during a disaster, it will be difficult to immediately alter the system structure in such a way as to restore the supply of electricity to all—or at least most—consumers.

The traditional structure of the electricity sector is transforming physically and institutionally in many countries for a variety of reasons, particularly in DMCs where access to electricity is often relatively low and where new stable models of electricity service are being implemented that give increased priority to utilization of clean and renewable power sources, including for rural electrification and for providing stable, self-generated power for industry. As such, a forward-looking response to a disaster affecting a power grid is not necessarily to replace or repair the infrastructure that has been damaged, but to consider what changes in electricity systems will yield a more robust, low-cost, and flexible system that will better meet future needs.

Build back better efforts should include the recovery and reconstruction of critical power infrastructure to meet higher standards of resilience to climate change and disaster events and, at the same time, leverage the current global and DMC energy transitions. These transitions are being driven by a range of factors, including national commitments to decarbonize energy sectors and increase the affordability of renewable energy and electricity storage systems. Economic and modal evolutions in the financing of renewable generation will result in greater variation in electricity supply options for consumers, in some cases displacing traditional power supply systems.

Recent nationally determined contributions prepared by developing countries include a number of activities focused on power system transition and long-term decarbonization. Such changes can be profound, as technologies that have been in place for decades (e.g., gas-, diesel-, or coal-fired electricity generation) are replaced with those that are new and operate on different principles. As such, power systems are now being planned and laid out differently as decentralization and distributed generation become more common. Rather than rely on a few large-scale power generation plants, there now may be an increased number of small-scale ones that are widely distributed and located closer to electricity loads. The ways in which energy is used also are significantly transforming, some traditionally fossil-fueled end uses starting to use electricity and electricity-derived renewable fuels such as hydrogen and ammonia. These energy changes will not only change end-uses in future electricity system designs but will provide ample BBB opportunities.

Recovery efforts, post-disaster, should provide higher standards of resilience to future natural hazards, leverage the transition of global energy systems, and take advantage of additional power sector objectives, particularly those described in Box 1. Post-disaster recovery and reconstruction of power systems may require consideration of various distinctive dynamics; these are outlined in Box 2.

Box 1: Key Objectives for Post-Disaster Recovery and Reconstruction of Power Systems

Global best practice studies and lessons learned from Asian Development Bank projects have shown that in addition to improving resilience, key objectives for reinstating power systems should include the following:

- **Accelerate the clean energy transition, reduce greenhouse gas emissions and air pollution, and increase energy independence** by leveraging and accelerating the use of renewable energy technologies, including cost-effective solar and wind generation; seizing opportunities to replace damaged end-use devices; and executing nationally determined contributions to support reconstruction and rehabilitation efforts.
- **Improve access and affordability** of power for end-users, particularly those in poor and vulnerable communities. Since renewable energy is often a less expensive source of electricity than fossil-fueled generation, it may be worth shifting to renewable generation even if subsidies are needed on a temporary basis to keep tariffs low.
- **Adopt new technologies (e.g., new electricity supply and/or energy storage and end-use technologies; new operation and business models)** that significantly contribute, in the long term, to power sector development and performance improvements. New technologies should be examined in the context of long-term utility planning to meet future energy and peak power needs, particularly in a changing physical and economic environment.

continued on next page

Box 1 *continued*

- **Generate new and more diverse livelihood opportunities** by enhancing skills and knowledge relating to the clean energy transition, including among utility staff; in ancillary industries such as suppliers and installers of power equipment, power generation, transmission, and distribution; and among clean energy users. This also promotes gender inclusion.
- **Enhance power system security** to reduce the risk of system attacks and damage by emerging digital threats.
- **Improve efficiency**, where possible, by installing the best available equipment when replacing damaged infrastructure, including efficient and low-emission transformers, upgraded cables, and other equipment, as well as built-in renewable energy systems.

Source: Asian Development Bank.

Box 2: Considerations for Delivering Power Sector Projects in a Post-Disaster Context

- **New players.** Following a disaster, there may be an influx of new stakeholders such as nongovernment organizations, philanthropists, and retailers that may subsidize and/or make available innovative technology services and systems, such as solar photovoltaic panels and equipment for rapid deployment, in order to temporarily restore local services while the wider grid is being repaired. A frenzy of activity with little coordination may take place, potentially impacting negatively on the market (e.g., prices slumping as a result of donations, which could reduce local market demand) thus hampering medium- and long-term prospects for shifting to sustainable and resilient electricity systems. These risks must be considered to ensure that power sector planning in the recovery stage includes a range of technologies (centralized as well as distributed) suitable for the public and private sectors and other key stakeholders, all of whom should be encouraged to provide input to ensure the long-term, built-back-better reliability of power systems.
- **Shifting landscape.** Even in the absence of a disaster, national electricity systems around the world are being pressured by advances in technology, such that reconstruction efforts should incorporate future-proofing to ensure resilience. In build back better efforts, restored energy systems should be redesigned so that they can better cope with a higher proportion of distributed and renewable energy. Since traditional standards and procedures in the installation and design of power generation, transmission, and distribution may no longer be adequate, the recovery period is an opportune time to install new technologies meeting higher standards. It is critical to understand how to safely install, connect, and operate the new technologies, and to provide the necessary support to build knowledge, skills, and capacities.
- **Barriers to change.** Following a disaster, there may be some power system operators that already have taken advantage of the shift toward clean energy, while some will continue to cling to traditional technologies and approaches. Existing power supply contracts, policy legislation, regulatory requirements, and current incentive structures (formal and/or informal) can all be barriers to change and can make it difficult for operators to embrace transition.
- **Changing consumption profiles.** Electrical consumption profiles are changing dramatically in concert with population growth, growth in gross domestic product, and emerging technologies. Historical data may not be sufficient to inform design, costing, or operational analyses of future energy needs, particularly during post-disaster electricity supply restoration.

continued on next page

Box 2 *continued*

- For example, in the Micronesia, Federated States of: Yap Renewable Energy Development Project (44469-013) of the Asian Development Bank, energy load had increased substantially by the time of project completion compared to forecasts and relative to actual demand estimates made four years earlier at project inception.[a] In build back better efforts, therefore, consumption profiles should be evaluated on the basis of the amount of electricity required and timing of power use, both of which can potentially vary over the coming decades.[b]

  Design assumptions should be clear with regard to load profiles so that the new or restored systems are able to reliably meet current and future demand and are constructed to allow for future expansion to meet greater loads.

- **Risk from digital attack.** The risk of a digital attack against new energy systems, including smart grids, may be greater than against traditional power grids due, in part, to added communication channels required to allow the balancing of electricity supply and demand. Post-disaster, this is of significant concern, particularly when security is overridden by the need to provide emergency services and ensure the rapid recovery of power, which increases digital vulnerability. Risks should be addressed through a variety of measures, including those typically have been applied to protect all communications over the internet.[c]

[a] ADB. 2019. *Completion Report: Yap Renewable Energy Development Project in the Federated States of Micronesia*.
[b] The timing and amount of electricity use affects system design, particularly when solar and/or wind power generation is used. This is due to the need to match the timing of peak power demand and overall electrical energy needs with the timing of electricity supplies from intermittent resources, often augmented with storage. The timing of electricity supply and demand must be considered during the reconstruction stage when designing capacity requirements of not only energy generation but also storage.
[c] Data breaches can be prevented by encryption, authentication, malware protection, network security through virtual private networks (VPN), remote access or site-to-site VPNs, and Network Intrusion Prevention System and Network Intrusion Detection System technologies. Regular risk assessments are essential to identify cybersecurity risks and methods to address them.

Source: Asian Development Bank.

ADB Tonga: Cyclone Gita Recovery Project (52129-001). Maintenance activities of energy infrastructure in Tonga. The Cyclone Gita Recovery Project reconstructed and climate- and disaster-proofed the Nuku'alofa electricity network that was damaged by Tropical Cyclone Gita in February 2018.

III

CLIMATE AND DISASTER RESILIENCE MEASURES

This section provides an overview of BBB measures to enhance the climate and disaster resilience of power sector projects during reconstruction and recovery following a disaster. It is based on a review of ADB emergency assistance activities and projects, staff consultations, and global best practice guidance.

Distributed Electricity Generation and Storage Technologies

Post-disaster recovery can provide an opportunity to achieve progress in the deployment and use of distributed energy technologies. Systems such as solar photovoltaic (PV) power, wind power, sustainably harvested biomass power, and/or mini- or micro-hydropower can supply a single household or set of households, while electricity can be stored in batteries or other advanced devices, as described below. Critical facilities such as hospitals, schools, water pumping systems, and key economic assets (e.g., factories and mines) can benefit from these technologies. Buildings and facilities either can possibly, given sufficient generation capacity and storage, be independent of the central grid or can be connected to the grid, but retaining the capacity for grid-independent operation in emergency situations.[7] System rebuild should enable the use of more grid-independent power sources so that (i) consumers are able to take control of their own energy supplies and expenses; and (ii) energy supplies are better retained during disasters, wherein buildings and facilities with operable power systems following disasters can help other households and service organizations in disaster recovery and in resuming operations.[8] A decentralized power system with fewer potential single points for failure tends to be more resilient to disasters.

---

[7]   The capacity for independent operation of grid-connected facilities typically requires special interconnection arrangements with the local utility or power provider.

[8]   Financial incentives may be needed to defray additional capital expenses associated with installing more disaster-resilient infrastructure.

Uptake of decentralized power generation plants that produce zero or low emissions should be encouraged to reduce local and greenhouse gas pollution, lower costs, and improve resilience to disasters and a changing climate, where such energy resources are available. ADB is able to liaise with government and private sector stakeholders to assist in identifying opportunities to create decentralized, low-emission power plants where economically viable.[9]

The design of decentralized low-emission facilities for power generation and storage should be such as to withstand future disasters and the impacts of climate change. With regard to distributed energy, for instance, plants should be able to transition from a grid-connected mode to an islanded mode where needed. Moreover, in the case of liquid- or gas-fueled generators, fuel storage and supply chains must be secured against the impacts of a disaster, regardless of whether fossil fuels or renewable fuels are used.

Key facilities including hospitals, health centers, and schools should be able to depend on temporary power connections post-disaster, in order to maintain an appropriate level of functionality of critical services. As such, selection of technologies and systems to replace damaged power systems should consider how solutions can be adapted for permanent installation as recovery efforts wind down. Similarly, households can be provided with attractive financing (e.g., grants and subsidies) to establish distributed energy systems that are able to adapt and expand to enable a permanent and reliable flow of electricity post-disaster.

The scale-up of distributed power generation to help the response to and recovery from future disasters is enabled by ensuring that the stock of distribution generation equipment can speedily be deployed, and that financial support and technical assistance are available for the uptake of distributed generation technologies in developing country markets. Policy-making support also should be provided to governments to encourage uptake, as should capacity building for system installation and maintenance.

Microgrid Technologies for Electricity Distribution in Local Areas

Distributed and decentralized energy devices such as those previously described can be linked by way of a microgrid—a localized group of interconnected loads and distributed energy resources within a clearly defined electrical boundary, such as a community (e.g., village, neighborhood, town, or city); educational or industrial campus; or mining installation. The localized group of loads acts as a single controllable entity with respect to the main regional or national electric grid (central or macrogrid). A related concept is the minigrid, which uses similar technologies and components, but is

---

[9]   This section refers primarily to power generation technology that produces low or no net greenhouse gas emissions, such as plants that rely on solar, wind, hydro, or sustainably produced biomass resources. It is possible, however, for some BBB efforts to call for a short-to-medium period where some fossil fuels (typically diesel, liquefied petroleum gas, or natural gas) might be needed as back-up for peaking units, or as energy to help meet demand during peak hours or to supplement renewable power while reconstruction is under way. Should fossil fuel be the option, units should be adaptable to the use of renewables (liquid or gas) in case of future similar circumstances.

at times defined as being grid-independent[10] Having the capability of being isolated from the main grid by a combination of smaller devices that more easily can be repaired, microgrids and minigrids are particularly well suited to rapid deployment following a disaster, as well as for maintaining and distributing electricity during or after the event. There are many examples whereby an islanded (independently operating) microgrid or minigrid is able to operate following a disaster event even when the wider network is inoperable.

Microgrids themselves can be made more resilient to disaster and climate challenges in a number of ways including by (i) physical protection (e.g., placing key facilities underground in cases where earthquake or geotechnical hazards are not the main concern, isolating them in well-secured shipping containers, or surrounding them by fences or berms); (ii) simplifying the temporary removal of vulnerable microgrid components in advance of an impending disaster; (iii) stockpiling back-up equipment items;[11] and (iv) using standard grid designs to facilitate return to operation following disasters.

Microgrids have been shown to dramatically improve the resilience of power networks to not only disasters but also to more routine hazards. In remote areas, islands, or where long transmission lines are necessary to supply relatively small loads, microgrids may be a more economical and efficient method to provide grid-quality electricity, compared to extending the centralized grid to that area. Microgrids are being used increasingly in BBB circumstances (Box 3) and even in communities where power has been supplied by a central grid for many decades.

Box 3: Project Example—Distributed Energy and Microgrids

Following the devastating dual impact of Hurricanes Irma and Maria in Puerto Rico in 2017 and the subsequent long-term power outages, distributed energy technologies (i.e., batteries, solar photovoltaic systems, and microgrids) were installed in some parts of the country through partnerships between the private sector and nongovernment organizations. The systems were usually placed around a particular community facility or resilience hub such as hospital, health center, or school.

Microgrids were key to restoring vital services to local communities and proved resilient against subsequent disasters, exemplified during the 2020 Puerto Rico earthquakes, where these particular sites ably and reliably continued to provide energy to their communities, while many islanders elsewhere suffered, yet again, from outages.

Sources: K. Adler. 2022. Puerto Rico Weighs Options for Expanding Renewable Power, Hardening Grid. HIS Markit. 9 April 2021; A. Kwasinski. 2018. Effects of Hurricane Maria on Renewable Energy Systems in Puerto Rico. Paper prepared for the 7th International Conference on Renewable Energy Research and Applications (ICRERA). 14–17 October, Paris; and M. Santos-Muñiz. 2019. 4 Energy Security Lessons from Rebuilding Puerto Rico's Electrical System after Hurricane Maria. *GreenBiz*. 27 September.

---

[10] The definition of microgrid and minigrid varies between publications, with some defining the two based on size, where the capacity of the microgrid is smaller than that of the minigrids. Others compare their function, whereby the minigrid is a fully functioning supply/demand system that operates independent of the main grid (e.g., in isolated areas or on islands) and the macrogrid is usually attached to a centralized grid but able to operate independently.

[11] As of this writing, although the full installed cost of solar PV is deemed to be $1,000 or more per kilowatt capacity, the cost of solar panel components to convert solar energy into electricity—the most physically vulnerable element of a solar PV—can be as low as $100 per kilowatt in bulk form from Alibaba.com. Extra panels, therefore, provide resilience against future disaster and are available to expand the microgrid as demand increases.

Energy Efficiency

It is widely recognized that the least expensive way to make more energy—including electricity—available is to improve the method by which the energy is converted into the energy service it provides. Examples include changing from incandescent or fluorescent bulbs to light-emitting diode (LED) bulbs; using more energy-efficient refrigerators, freezers, and air conditioning units; and utilizing above-standard-efficiency industrial and agricultural motors, pumps, and processing equipment. In the wake of a disaster, a modest additional cost outlay to replace damaged devices and equipment with higher-efficiency units will yield substantial and sustained dividends (such as reduced electricity costs) to consumers, as well as reduced system costs for power operators. In some cases, substituting renewable, nonelectric sources of energy in place of electric devices (e.g., solar water heaters replacing electric water heaters) also will reduce power needs and costs.

Conceivably, certain kinds of technology devices, for example, electric vehicles (EVs) can be classified as both supply and energy-efficient demand devices, not only in post-disaster situations but also routinely. An EV is a more efficient and cost-effective means of transport than a vehicle using gasoline (petrol), or diesel, and can be easily charged by portable and emergency renewable power sources if there is a break in the supply of liquid fuel as a result of a disaster event. The batteries in EVs can also be used to store power from renewable energy systems for use in restoring critical energy services following a disaster.

A further benefit of energy-efficient equipment during post-disaster recovery is that there is less energy used—for instance, the more efficient the device or equipment, the less power generation plant, substations, transmission and distribution (T&D), infrastructure, electricity storage, and fuel storage will be necessary, because the required capacity to meet power demand will be lower.[12] Additionally, the same supply-side investment can support more users following a disaster if higher-efficiency end-use devices are installed.

A further means to reduce the cost of electricity following a disaster is to introduce demand reduction measures, for example to enable micro- or central grid operators to optimize consumer power usage to ensure available generation can meet demand, and/or reduce the cost of generation during peak demand. The use of demand control can allow available electricity services to be provided to more people immediately following a disaster, and for system costs (and costs to consumers) to be reduced as routine operations are resumed.

---

[12]   E. Long. 2020. *Microgrids for Resilience, Yes. But Don't Overlook Their Efficiency Potential*. *Alliance to Save Energy*. 10 September.

Resilient Transmission and Distribution Systems

In many cases, resilient energy technologies like underground cables have proven uneconomical for widespread use resulting in mostly aboveground T&D systems that have been more prone to failure in disaster conditions than they could have been. More recent technologies (e.g., bundled aerial conductors), however, are more capable of withstanding certain hazards and tend to be less expensive to install. Resilient bundled aerial conductors, for example, may better withstand falling trees and winds than can typical uninsulated conductors. Nevertheless, bundled aerial conductors remain as vulnerable as traditional above-ground T&D systems to other modes of distribution system failure such as damage to distribution poles and towers when adequate resilience measures are not included in the design.

Other options to improve T&D system resilience include

(i)   adding distributed grid storage;
(ii)   placing key T&D system components underground and/or away from hazard;
(iii)   replacing damaged power lines with more meshed configurations;[13]
(iv)   clearing vegetation away from power lines;
(v)   hardening T&D systems, including installing stronger T&D towers and placing critical lines underground (see Box 8 for a full case study on ADB's support for a resilient power network in Tonga);
(vi)   implementing smart grid features, e.g., sensors, communications and control equipment; and
(vii)   introducing protocols and software tools to allow grid operators to not only diagnose grid issues sooner during a disaster, but also to be able to isolate trouble spots along the grid.

The cost–benefit analysis of strengthening infrastructure during reconstruction may need to be revisited to account for the impacts of a changing climate. It may be more economically feasible to place electricity supply lines to critical loads or to feed critical circuits underground, as long as there is up-to-date recognition of the potential impacts of disaster effects (damage and loss) and climate change. Some of the resilience measures noted previously may be more costly than standard practice. If introduced immediately to prevent power outage, they easily will pay for themselves when a disaster occurs. When life-cycle costs are considered, these measures can become cost-effective over the design life because of the reduction in the repair costs and supply interruptions to power systems when future natural hazard events occur.

Increasingly, power sector agencies and utilities are seeking to take a more comprehensive approach to evaluate potential resilience priorities for T&D systems as part of the BBB process. An example for Tonga is provided in Box 4.

---

[13]   Vision of a future meshed network is provided in C. Liu and E.M. Stewart. 2021. *Electricity Transmission System Research and Development: Distribution Integrated with Transmission Operations*. *White Papers*. United States Department of Energy.

> ### Box 4: Project Example—Resilient Transmission and Distribution and Analytical Tools
>
> In 2014, under the Asian Development Bank Tonga: Cyclone Ian Recovery Project[a] (48192-001),
> the Ha'apai electricity network was reconstructed and climate- and disaster-proofed by reconnecting an
> underground cable to 1,010 households and 27 commercial and government consumers. A 1.5-kilometer
> high-voltage underground cable was constructed to service the new public hospital in Lifuka.
>
> The Tonga Office of Electricity, North American Transmission Forum, Electric Power Research Institute,
> and Pacific Northwest National Laboratory (the latter three in the United States) collaborated to develop
> the new Transmission Resilience Maturity Model.[b] This software tool enables utilities to "evaluate and
> benchmark" the maturity of their transmission resilience programs and to increase the resilience of their
> transmission systems. The Transmission Resilience Maturity Model evaluates a utility's strategies, policies,
> and procedures and the implementation of programmatic activities to support resilience.
>
> [a] ADB. Tonga: Cyclone Ian Recovery Project.
> [b] Transmission Resilience Maturity Model. 2022. Strengthen your Transmission Resilience. Version 1.0.
>
> Source: Asian Development Bank.

Relocatable and Customizable Systems

Traditional power system design and regulatory approaches tend to focus on "permanent" equipment
installations. Although such approaches aim to provide reliable long-term energy supply, they may
result in more service interruption by exposing equipment to greater levels of disaster risk, as they are
substantially difficult to relocate or customize in response to disaster.

An alternative approach is to install demountable or transportable equipment not only for use during
disaster recovery but also for the longer term, when it can be moved out of harm's way prior to an
extreme weather event and brought back post-disaster (Box 5). Although demounting the equipment
may temporarily interrupt power transmission in the area it is serving, power can be restored far more
quickly than if the equipment had been damaged. Wind turbines, solar generation stations, battery
storage, and some fossil-fueled generators are designed to be demountable or transportable. These
technologies are likely to be more suited to BBB efforts in islanded communities, remote areas, or
where there are relatively low loads, and they have the advantage of being available for future disaster
relief. Several companies have developed complete solar PV systems, including panels, batteries,
inverters, and other ancillary equipment, able to be transported in shipping containers and deployed in
a matter of hours.[14]

---

[14] An example of one of the self-contained PV or battery systems is described in Brisbane Water. 2022. Introducing
the Ecos PowerCube. Other examples of container-based or container-mounted systems of various designs and
capacities include, but certainly are not limited to, folding systems developed by (i) PWRstation (E. Bellini. 2021.
Containerized, Retractable PV System for Quick Deployment. *PV Magazine*. 28 May) and (ii) microgrid systems
delivered in and deployed on a shipping container (BoxPower. 2022. SolarContainer).

ADB Federated States of Micronesia: Yap Renewable Energy Development Project (44469-013). The project included three 275-kilowatt demountable wind turbines that can be tilted to the ground ahead of an extreme weather event and thus avoid damage.

The Asian Development Bank approved the Micronesia, Federated States of: Yap Renewable Energy Development Project (44469-013) in June 2013 for $11.2 million. The project supported the Yap State Public Services Commission—the public utility responsible for power generation in the state—in developing renewable energy and ensuring stronger supply-side energy efficiency of the electricity grid.

While the project was not delivered in a post-disaster context, in recognition of the high risk of tropical cyclones in the area, the project included three 275-kilowatt demountable wind turbines that can be tilted to the ground ahead of an extreme weather event and thus avoid damage; these can be reinstalled easily when storms have passed.

Source: ADB. Micronesia, Federated States of: Yap Renewable Energy Development Project.

Resilient Equipment Standards

After a disaster, model standards can be adopted to ensure resilient, safe, and continued operation of new equipment. Many of the new technologies involved in the energy transition that should be supported by BBB have substantially varying requirements for their safe installation and operation compared to the technologies they replace. Electricity sector structures, equipment, and power lines built or rebuilt in the wake of a disaster should conform to modern standards (and their respective normative requirements for addressing natural hazards) to help ensure that the abilities of these types of infrastructure to survive future disasters are strong. Many of these standards also offer co-benefits, such as better occupational safety for electricity sector workers, raising the safety level for electricity users, boosting environmental performance, and reducing electricity loss.

In some cases, updated in-country standards, procedures, and guidelines to assist with the safe installation and operation of new technology may not be available in DMCs. As such, adopting best practice standards from other countries may be appropriate if no regulatory barriers exist.[15] Adoption by DMCs of international best practices and standards for electricity sector infrastructure will make it easier for vendors within and outside the country to provide equipment and services that are compliant with regulations. Improving building codes (which should also include building energy codes; see Box 6) may be a start so that during reconstruction, equipment or buildings comply with international standards such as those of the Institute of Electrical and Electronics Engineers,[16] the European Union, North America, or Australia and New Zealand. Care should be taken, however, to guarantee that the types of equipment, buildings, and structures installed are consistent with local needs.

Box 6: Project Examples—Resilient Standards

As part of the Asian Development Bank (ADB) 2005 Pakistan: Earthquake Emergency Assistance Project (39631-013), power infrastructure was reconstructed according to newly introduced building codes for the affected area and was made more earthquake-resistant. Where possible, multihazard-resistant standards were instituted to improve resilience against flood, wind, and landslide.

ADB's Tonga: Cyclone Gita Recovery Project (52129-001) applied the latest technical standards from Australia and New Zealand to enhance resilience of reconstructed power infrastructure, given the lack of appropriate local standards.

Sources: ADB. Pakistan: Earthquake Emergency Assistance Project; and ADB. Tonga: Cyclone Gita Recovery Project.

System Dependencies

Sector recovery planning following a disaster provides a key opportunity to identify and protect the dependencies within and among energy infrastructure, energy services, and power systems particularly with dependencies with other critical infrastructure (e.g., hospitals, electric transport systems, evacuation centers, water/water treatment plants, and telecommunication providers). To ignore these relationships may significantly degrade system resilience and impede the speed of recovery following a disaster. Key opportunities to enhance the resilience of electricity-dependent systems are meant to (i) provide for independent, possibly redundant, power supplies and/or storage to meet essential needs; (ii) replace damaged wiring systems in buildings, such as hospitals, clinics, emergency response facilities and schools so as to isolate key functions (e.g., emergency lighting, refrigeration, and triage centers); and (iii) retain some back-up transport equipment when rebuilding electric transport systems (consistent with goals of the energy transition) that can be powered by fossil or renewable fuels in case electric transport is interrupted in a future disaster.

---

[15]   Examples include the Australian/New Zealand Standard 4777.2 and Standard 5132 on modern inverter and battery installation, or the International Electrotechnical Commission Standard 62133 and Standard 62281 on battery installation and transport.

[16]   See, for example, IEEE. 2022. Standards.

Much of today's electricity generation and T&D technology requires telecommunication networks to interconnect with control and monitoring systems, while certain thermal power systems depend on the supply of water for cooling. Emergency generators, equipment parts, and fuel may need to be transported by road or rail, which means that roads and rail lines have to be passable, operable, and/or immediately repaired following disruption as a result of disaster. The next disaster will be easier to recover from if, by BBB, these system interdependencies are optimized for fast recovery or are minimized. Further up the logistics network, interruptions in the supply of fuel may cause electricity generation systems to become inoperable due, for example, to liquid fuel or gas pipeline rupture; berthing facility, fuel storage tank, and fuel (gas or oil) refinery damage; coal mine inundation; and fuel handling equipment or coal storage center destruction.[17]

Build back better efforts should address power system vulnerabilities that may stem from the interconnection of critical power sector infrastructure and other systems. Identifying critical dependencies between power and other systems is an important first step to ensure that dependencies are protected and provide diverse back-up systems to avoid loss of operation across connected sectors. For example, robust transport access routes are essential for the delivery of repair supplies, fuel, and emergency generators to restore power infrastructure. Minimizing dependence on imported fuels can help improve continuity when transport systems and supply chains are disrupted. An example of system interdependency is showcased in Box 7, which describes the backup generation systems following the Great East Japan Earthquake of 2011.

Power Sector Control, Monitoring, and Modeling Systems

Power systems in many countries have suffered from underinvestment; in some cases, they lag in adopting modern methods of electricity sector management, monitoring, and use of modeling systems that would contribute to rapid and resilient power grid recovery following disaster. Control systems are also crucial in enabling a power grid to accommodate larger fractions of intermittent renewable electricity sources and their associated systems. Post-disaster reconstruction offers an opportunity to accelerate the use of a range of smart grid technologies, (e.g., central grid and remotely operated power plant and T&D system controls), as well as control hardware and software providing real-time operational information from end-user facilities to the central grid.

Following a disaster, the components of the power grid should not only be rebuilt using more modern generation systems and T&D equipment, but the system also should be upgraded to allow more convenient and rapid monitoring and modelling of grid performance. Improvements in grid modeling will help in responding to future disasters as well as enable a transition to cleaner sources of electricity. Raising the effectiveness of central grid energy management and upgrading related systems, however, may require significant time and expense, particularly in building DMC capacities to effectively adapt to and use upgraded and updated technology.

---

[17]   VietnamPlus. 2015. Thermal Power Plants May Face Coal Shortage: Quang Ninh Province's Historic Rainstorm this Week Severely Disrupted the Area's Coal Supplies and Could Temporarily Shut Down Several Thermal Power Plants. 31 July.

Box 7: Failure of Critical Systems in a Disaster Due to Interdependency

In the Great East Japan Earthquake of 2011, many of the backup generation systems installed to ensure reliability of electricity supply, including to a main water treatment plant in Sendai City, ultimately failed when the supply of diesel fuel for the generators was interrupted as a result of extensive damage to the regional road network.[a] The same disaster damaged several reactors of the Fukushima Daiichi Nuclear Power Plant, and due to the failure of diesel-fuel backup generators to draw cooling water from the ocean, the power plant's fuel overheated and the reactor core melted. The failure of the backup cooling pumps, however, was not due to a lack of access to fuel supplies, but rather the fact that the pumps were situated at a low elevation on the coastline, which was inundated by the tsunami that followed the earthquake. This event underscores the need for safe placement of backup generators, not only in the case of power plants but also in relation to other facilities while keeping the impacts of disaster in mind.

The New Orleans power distribution system nearly collapsed following the devastating impact of Hurricane Katrina in 2005. Impacts related to the loss of electricity cascaded to health services, transportation, and law enforcement. Within the distribution network, however, the power supply for the flood pumping system was partially independent and able to relieve the city from floodwater, albeit over a number of weeks, while the central power was being restored. Lessons from this event have contributed to a shift toward efforts to decentralize and increase redundancy within power networks in the United States.[b]

[a] K. Sawada et al. n.d. *Countermeasures Against a Long-term Blackout in Sendai City Waterworks Bureau Passed Through the Great East Japan Earthquake.*
[b] Lloyds. 2017. *Emerging Risk Report 2017—Society and Security: Future Cities: Building Infrastructure Resilience.*

Source: Asian Development Bank.

Power Sector Capacity Building

The education and skills required to operate a modern power system continue to evolve as energy systems, in general—and power systems in particular—transition to clean energy sources. Although many distributed energy technologies (e.g., rooftop solar PV) can be installed by those with specific, albeit limited, job training, other features of the clean energy transition (as with other types of resilient energy systems) will require considerable capacity building to effectively establish and operate the new systems. Operation of power systems with extensive distributed energy technology, for example, can be complex and, in many ways, is approached quite differently compared to traditional centralized power systems. Post-disaster reconstruction efforts should therefore include capacity building to ensure that system hardware and software can be operated and maintained effectively.

Many DMCs have limited capacity to design and build distributed power systems, let alone the knowledge to operate the necessary software and hardware. In BBB, it is important to ensure that the skills of power system operators, maintenance personnel, power sector planners and regulators, and other stakeholders are up to date with the rollout of new and more resilient technologies and software, as well as with best practices to effectively plan, operate, and maintain power systems in the long term for climate change and disaster resilience. Acquiring and retaining all of these capabilities will require professional training, in country and off site. Examples of training programs integrated in post-disaster assistance are included in Box 8. Capacity building can be consumer-focused so as to raise awareness to improve energy efficiency; reduce energy consumption and greenhouse gas emissions; and encourage the use of renewable energy systems. The outcome will be twofold: not only will more people be served as power systems are restored, but progress toward energy transition objectives also will be achieved.

Finally, the capacities of DMCs in energy planning, in general—and in power sector planning in particular—need to be developed. Energy planning in the BBB process will help to gradually shift DMC power sectors to clean energy, given that future energy systems will continue to evolve. For utilities— whether state-owned, municipal, or privately owned—training in long-range planning techniques will help utility planners to assess national or regional electricity system options.[18] Education in the use of more detailed generation expansion planning using various types of models and data also may be required. As distributed energy systems, including microgrids, become more relevant in extending electricity services to rural areas and providing reliable, resilient power to communities and critical services, further training will be needed for those who will develop and regulate the electricity markets for small and large power producers.

Box 8: Project Example—Enhancing Resilience of Tonga's Power System

Tonga is a nation of 176 islands and is one of the most vulnerable countries in the world to disasters triggered by natural hazards. Tropical Cyclone Ian damaged over 90% of the electricity network on the Ha'apai island group in 2014, leaving most of the area and 5,000 people without power. Severe Tropical Cyclone Gita (TC Gita) made landfall on 12 February 2018 as the most intense storm to ever strike the country. TC Gita caused widespread destruction on the islands of Tongatapu and 'Eua, damaging or destroying nearly 5,000 houses and many public buildings, and leaving customers without power. Total energy sector recovery cost as a result was approximately $45.9 million. In late 2019 and 2020 alone, three more tropical cyclones struck Tonga: Sarai, Tino, and Harold. Then, in early 2022, the volcano bridging the islands of Hunga Tonga and Hunga Ha'apai erupted, affecting an estimated four-fifths of the nation's population, causing a tsunami, and blanketing the main island of Tongatapu and other islands in the archipelago with ash.[a]

Tonga's electricity system had previously faced significant challenges. In 2008, the formerly private-owned power generation, transmission, and distribution network was in disrepair, and with 100% of the island's electricity supply generation relying on diesel fuel, the cost to the customer (tariffs) was at a record high. That same year, Tonga took back control of the electricity system and formed Tonga Power Ltd. (TPL). With support from the Asian Development Bank (ADB) and other development partners, TPL—in collaboration with other Tongan agencies—prepared an Energy Road Map. This included a 10-year plan to reduce Tonga's exposure to the price of oil by supplying 50% of electricity from renewable energy sources, enhancing disaster resilience, and initiating projects to overhaul the power system.[b] The road map informed efficient and rapid identification of climate and disaster resilience investments following the tropical cyclones.[c]

continued on next page

---

[18]   Planning should include demand forecasting, supply- and demand-side resources and technologies, and climate change adaptation and mitigation methods. Furthermore, planning should include stakeholder involvement (Integrated Resource Planning).

Box 8 *continued*

Following TC Gita, ADB[d] and the Government of New Zealand[e] approved separate grants to help reconstruct and improve disaster resilience of the Nuku'alofa electricity network, in partnership with Tonga and TPL. Recovery efforts in the build back better (BBB) context included building a more decentralized, low-carbon energy system with strengthened distribution assets. Specific resilience measures included the following:

- Move service connections (the link between a building and the street electricity network) underground for a large number of houses and commercial and government buildings.
- Change distribution system aerial conductors from individual-wired lines to bundled lines, improving their resistance to damage and ensuring that restoration of future outages can be made rapidly. The time it will take to restore bundled aerial conductors is estimated to be one-third of the time it takes to restore the existing open wire system.
- Upgrade the capacity of the distribution network, including medium- and low-voltage conductors and associated distribution transformers, to cope with future load changes.
- Construct high-voltage underground supply lines to critical loads such as hospitals.
- Reconfigure the network to better manage voltage, facilitating the addition of more renewable energy supplies.
- Apply the latest norms from Standards Australia and Standards New Zealand when performing network upgrades and repairs.
- Establish gender inclusiveness in project consultations and planning, as well as in the electricity sector workforce, thus expanding community awareness of electricity sector issues and diversifying the workforce—one that is better equipped to respond to disaster.

The strategic road map to modernize and strengthen the resilience of the power system will benefit Tonga significantly in responding to future disasters. Network upgrades, furthermore, will improve reliability, as evidenced by the remarkable drop in the number of outages following subsequent cyclones. For example, approximately only 5% of the upgraded power grids in Tongatapu and 'Eua were damaged following TC Gita, compared to around 45% in other areas.[f] ADB continues to support Tonga's national energy resilience through its 2019 Tonga Renewable Energy Project.[g]

ADB Tonga: Cyclone Gita Recovery Project (52129-001). Maintenance activities of energy infrastructure in Tonga. The Cyclone Gita Recovery Project reconstructed and climate- and disaster-proofed the Nuku'alofa electricity network that was damaged by Tropical Cyclone Gita in February 2018.

continued on next page

Box 8 *continued*

Resilient upgrade of distribution systems. Left: Original open-wire distribution system; right: a new and more resilient aerial-bundled conductor (photos by Tonga Power Ltd.).

The BBB efforts have contributed to faster restoration of the country's energy supply in subsequent cyclones. Based on the strength of TC Gita, restoration was estimated to have required two months, but was actually completed in five weeks. Following TC Harold in April 2020, service was restored within six days. Nevertheless, there is still room for continued improvement.

In addition to strengthening Tonga's power system resilience and improving its cost effectiveness, BBB efforts have brought other advantages to the country. One such example is that by improving gender diversity in the workplace, TPL has established an all-female line working crew.[h]

[a] See, for example, BBC News. 2022. *Tonga Volcano: Eruption More Powerful than Atomic Bomb, NASA Says*. 7 January.
[b] Kingdom of Tonga. 2010. *Tonga Energy Road Map 2010–2020*. Nuku-alofa; ADB. *Tonga: Outer Island Renewable Energy Project*; and ADB. *Tonga: Cyclone Ian Recovery Project*.
[c] P. Tohi. n.d. *Tonga Renewable Energy Roadmap*. Tonga Power Ltd., Nuku'alofa.
[d] ADB. *Tonga: Cyclone Gita Recovery Project*.
[e] Government of New Zealand. 2018. *NZ Supports Tonga Recovery Effort Post Cyclone*. 7 March.
[f] ADB. 2018. *Report and Recommendation of the President to the Board of Directors: Proposed Grant to the Kingdom of Tonga for the Cyclone Gita Recovery Project*.
[g] ADB. 2019. *Pacific Renewable Energy Investment Facility: Proposed Grant to the Kingdom of Tonga for the Renewable Energy Project*.
[h] ADB. 2019. *Tonga: As Part of Renewable Energy and Gender Push, All-Woman Crew Restores Powerlines*. 16 September.

Source: Asian Development Bank.

ADB Federated States of Micronesia: Yap Renewable Energy Development Project (44469-013).
The project included three 275-kilowatt demountable wind turbines that can be tilted to the ground
ahead of an extreme weather event and thus avoid damage.

SUGGESTED READINGS

The following technical and subject matter resources are further references in implementing nonstructural build back better measures.

Asian Development Bank (ADB). 2013. Guidelines for Climate Proofing Investment in the Energy Sector.

ADB. 2022. Making Urban Power Distribution Systems Climate Resilient.

A. Kwasinski. 2018. Effects of Hurricane Maria on Renewable Energy Systems in Puerto Rico. Paper prepared for the 7th International Conference on Renewable Energy Research and Applications. Paris. 14–17 October.

M. Santos-Muñiz. 2019. 4 Energy Security Lessons from Rebuilding Puerto Rico's Electrical System after Hurricane Maria. GreenBiz. 27 September.

C. Liu and E.M. Stewart. 2021. Electricity Transmission System Research and Development: Distribution Integrated with Transmission Operations. Paper prepared for the Office of Electricity, United States Department of Energy Transmission Innovation Symposium: Modernizing the US Electric Grid. 2021 White Papers. April.

Transmission Resilience Maturity Model. 2021. Strengthen your Transmission Resilience (20 November).

Institute of Electrical and Electronics Engineers (IEEE) Power and Energy Society. Standards.

K. Sawada et. al. Japan Water Works Association. Countermeasures against a Long-term Blackout in Sendai City Waterworks Bureau Passed Through the Great East Japan Earthquake.

Lloyd's and Arup. 2017. Future Cities: Building infrastructure Resilience. In Emerging Risk Report 2017, Society and Security. United States Cybersecurity and Infrastructure Security Agency. Resilient Power Best Practices for Critical Facilities and Sites with Guidelines, Analysis, Background Material, and References.